C
629.224
3-96

D0913005

WORK TRUCKS

HEAVY EQUIPMENT

David and Patricia Armentrout

The Rourke Book Co., Inc.
Vero Beach, Florida 32964

RALSTON PUBLIC LIBRARY
7900 PARK LANE
RALSTON, NEB. 68127

© 1995 The Rourke Book Co., Inc.

All rights reserved. No part of this book may be reproduced or utilized in any form or by any means, electronic or mechanical including photocopying, recording or by any information storage and retrieval system without permission in writing from the publisher.

PHOTO CREDITS
© CASE: page 7; © East Coast Studios: Cover, Title page, pages 4, 8, 10, 12, 13, 15, 17, 18; © NASA page 21

Library of Congress Cataloging-in-Publication Data

Armentrout, Patricia, 1960-
    Work trucks / by Patricia Armentrout and David Armentrout.
        p. cm. — (Heavy Equipment)
    Includes index.
    ISBN 1-55916-132-9
    1. Trucks—Juvenile literature.   [1. Trucks.]
I. Armentrout, David, 1962-   .   II. Title.   III. Series: Armentrout,
Patricia, 1960-   Heavy Equipment.
TL230.15.A76 1995
629.224—dc20   95–3980
                                                                      CIP
                                                                       AC

Printed in the USA

TABLE OF CONTENTS

Rewibe $9.95 10-95

WORK TRUCKS

Work trucks are the most common types of heavy equipment. They are used every day in almost every kind of business.

Work trucks can be as small as a family pick-up or as large as an 18-wheel **tractor-trailer** (TRAK ter-TRAY ler).

We see many of the common work trucks every day, but some work trucks are used for special jobs. They may not even look like a truck at all.

When the power goes out, workers use
lift trucks to repair the traffic lights

DUMP TRUCKS

Dump trucks carry dirt, gravel, sand, and trash. Almost anything that can be dumped without being damaged can be hauled in a dump truck.

Construction companies, **mining** (MY ning) companies, and gravel companies all use big powerful dump trucks.

The biggest dump truck weighs over 84 tons, or 168,000 pounds! It is too big to be driven on public roads, but it is at home in a rock **quarry** (KWOR ree) or coal mine.

Dump trucks are used to remove dirt and rock from work sites

SNOW PLOWS

There are many types of snow plows, but the most common is a dump truck with a plow mounted on the front.

This type of snow plow is very useful. The heavy truck can easily push the snow off the road. It also carries a load of salt.

As the plow clears the snow from the road, salt and sand are dumped or spread evenly over the road's surface. The salt melts the ice and small amounts of snow that the plow has missed.

Snow plows clear snow-covered roads to allow for safer travel

TOW TRUCKS

Cars and trucks make it easier to get from one place to another. When cars and trucks break down, a tow truck driver is called. Tow trucks are sometimes called wreckers because they often tow wrecked cars and trucks.

Most tow trucks attach a tow bar to the front of the broken down vehicle. The vehicle is then pulled to a nearby auto garage for repair.

Some tow trucks carry broken down vehicles on their beds. Others have such powerful engines that they can tow a tractor-trailer.

Tow trucks are used when cars and trucks break down or run out of gas

11

RALSTON PUBLIC LIBRARY
7900 PARK LANE
RALSTON, NEB. 68127

This dump truck is being loaded with large concrete and brick pieces

Utility trucks are used when bad weather damages power lines

CEMENT TRUCKS

You have probably seen big trucks with revolving barrels driving down the road or parked at a construction site. These unusual trucks are called cement trucks.

Cement trucks do two jobs at one time. As the barrel turns it mixes sand, water, and clay to make cement. At the same time it transports the mixture to a construction site.

The truck slowly pours its cement down a chute at the back of the truck. When the cement dries, it will be very hard and strong. Cement may be mixed with gravel to make it even stronger. This mix is called concrete.

A sidewalk is made of concrete poured from a cement truck

GARBAGE TRUCKS

You can probably guess what a garbage truck is used for. Garbage trucks carry garbage or trash to dumps or **disposal** (dis POE zul) sites.

Garbage is loaded into a large hopper, or opening, at the rear of the truck. After the garbage is dumped into the hopper, a blade crushes and pushes the garbage towards the front of the truck.

Some garbage trucks are made to lift large metal trash containers called dumpsters. The dumpster can then be turned to drop its load into the truck.

16 *Some garbage trucks are made to lift large metal dumpsters*

TRACTOR-TRAILERS

Tractor-trailers are the most common type of work truck. They are used for long-distance hauling.

The tractor does most of the work. It has a powerful engine and can pull heavy loads. Some tractors have sleeping compartments for the driver, which is helpful on long trips.

The trailer is pulled by the tractor. The trailer can be loaded with just about anything. Trailors hold hundreds of boxes. Some trailers are large tanks that hold liquids; others are refrigerated to haul food.

A tractor-trailer with a flat bed can haul oversized equipment

THE CRAWLER/TRANSPORTER

Some trucks are built for one special purpose. One of these special trucks was built for **NASA** (NASA). It is called a Crawler/Transporter.

The Crawler/Transporter is a huge machine. It weighs over 5 million pounds and is used to carry rockets from their **hangar** (HANG er) to the launch pad.

The Crawler/Transporter rides on treads and moves very slowly. It goes only one mile per hour at top speed! You may have seen the Crawler/Transporter carry a space shuttle to a launch pad.

20   *The space shuttle is taken to the launch pad on the NASA crawler/transporter*

WHY DO WE NEED WORK TRUCKS?

Trucks transport food from one part of the country to the other. They make it possible for people in the northeast to have oranges from Florida in January and broccoli from California in March.

Work trucks help build the houses we live in, the highways we drive on, and the businesses we work in.

Without work trucks it would be impossible to live the lifestyle of today. Notice how many types of trucks you see that affect the way we live.

Glossary

disposal (dis POE zul) — the act of getting rid of, throwing out

hangar (HANG er) — a covered area for airship housing and repair

mining (MY ning) — removing minerals from the earth

NASA (NASA) — National Aeronautics and Space Administration

quarry (KWOR ree) — a large hole in the earth for mining building stone, like limestone and slate

tractor-trailer (TRAK ter-TRAY ler) — a hauling vehicle that has an engine tractor pulling a hauling compartment trailer

INDEX